JUMP STARTS FOR CATECHISTS

The Prayer Journey

ALISON BERGER

The Prayer Journey

Twenty-Third Publications
A Division of Bayard
185 Willow Street
P.O. Box 180
Mystic, CT 06355
(860) 536-2611 or (800) 321-0411
www.twentythirdpublications.com
ISBN:1-58595-514-0

Contents

About This Series

The *Jump Starts for Catechists* series offers catechists
   quick, hands-on tips for their faith formation sessions.
Each booklet provides practical and "classroom-tested"
   information, formation, and ideas
   that are valuable for beginning
      as well as experienced catechists.
The books are written by some of
   Twenty-Third Publications' best-selling authors,
   including Gwen Costello, Sr. Mary Kathleen Glavich,
      Dan Connors, and Alison Berger.
Other books available in this series include
   Stories That Teach, *The Liturgical Year*, and *The Early Church*.

The Prayer Journey

The single most important factor in your life
   and the lives of your children and teens
      is your relationship with God.
One name we give that relationship is prayer.
The Prayer Journey covers basic areas of the prayer relationship.
It provides the theology, background, methodology,
   and techniques to help catechists more effectively guide
      their learners in their prayer life.
Since the primary means for achieving this
   is through the catechists' own example,
   The Prayer Journey is also an invaluable guide for catechists
      in their own relationship with God.

Introduction

I've often noticed in my own family and in religion classes
   that children are, in a real sense, naturally inclined to prayer
      and to spiritual realities.
They feel the presence of God in and around them,
   without being able to express it as such.
As catechists you have the privilege and responsibility
   to assist them in developing and directing that inclination.
The purpose of this booklet is to provide some background,
   guidelines, and techniques that can help you as catechists
      more effectively guide your children in their life of prayer.

What is the primary means for fulfilling that responsibility?
You, of course, through your example.
So another purpose of this booklet
   is to be a guide for you
   in deepening your own prayer life.
We will consider what prayer is and some practical ways
   of communicating it.
We will examine the sources of our prayer.
Together we will look at prayer in Scripture—
   especially in the life of Jesus, our example in prayer—
   and at prayer in the Church's liturgy.
Finally we will reflect on the Our Father,
   the prayer Jesus taught us and the model for all prayer.
As we consider each of these topics, we will discuss ideas
   for applying them in your religion class.

At the end of each chapter is a prayer experience
    you can share with your learners,
        as well as questions for reflection and discussion.
All of these may help you delve more deeply
    into the content of this booklet
        and apply it in your ministry and life.

CHAPTER ONE

What Is Prayer?

My niece Victoria used to spend one day a week
    with grandma and grandpa,
        and each enjoyed the other's company.
This particular day my mother was looking for Vicki;
    the house was very quiet.
Mom was becoming a little anxious until she saw the child
    kneeling in a corner near the large statue of Mary
        that was in the bay window.
"What are you doing, Vicki?" my mother asked.
"I'm praying," the four-year-old replied.

Children, especially the very young, can impress us
    with the simplicity and naturalness of their prayer.
They need guidance, however, in developing and directing
    their inclination to pray.
While the family is the primary place for this formation,
    catechists can and do play an important role as well.

Where Do We Start?

Let's look at our understanding of prayer
  and how we can communicate what prayer is
    in a religious education setting.
Not too long ago my friends and I
  were discussing this very topic.
One said, "I think prayer is something very personal
  between me and God.
If I have a problem, I ask God for help.
If I've done something wrong,
  I feel as though I've hurt a close friend.
I try to share this personal aspect with my kids."
Another said it's important for children to learn
  at least some basic prayer formulas,
    according to their age level.
Others pointed out the need for prayer
  as a faith community.
Everyone agreed that real prayer is two-way communication,
  like talking with a close friend.
What does it mean, talking with a close friend?
I don't know about you, but I share just about everything
  with my best friend: my ups and downs,
    my successes and bloopers, my dreams and fears.
How can I do that?
  Because of the relationship we have, the trust we share.
Our God calls each of us—catechists and children—
  to an even deeper relationship than that.
In fact, in the book of Isaiah God tells us,
  "I have called you by name, you are mine." (Is 43:1)
St. Augustine expressed beautifully our response to that call:
  "Our hearts are restless, Lord, until they rest in you."
Prayer, then, is our relationship with God,
  our response of faith and love to God's love.

We want to impart this to our learners,
  especially by our natural manner of praying
    and of talking about God.

A Cry of Love

Prayer is a "surge of the heart," wrote St. Thérèse of Lisieux.
"It is a simple look turned toward heaven;
  it is a cry of recognition and love."
Real prayer comes from the heart,
  from the center of our being.
I withdraw there when I want to meet God,
  whether in meditation, in a brief prayer moment,
    a recognition of God's presence, or thanksgiving.
The children I've taught—even the youngest—
  enjoy simple guided meditations,
    even some personal quiet time.
We've used such meditations on different occasions,
  either to begin or end a session, or to mark a special event
    such as a birthday or a holyday.
One of my friends told me that her sixth graders
  like to keep a journal.
She often allots ten minutes at the end of a religion session
  to give them time to think and write
  about what they've learned and discussed
    so they can talk to God about it.
God leads each person on his or her own path of prayer.
Each person responds according to the call in their own heart.
So when we teach about prayer, or even when we lead prayer,
  we need to let the children and teens follow their own way.
The ability to listen is important for our growth in prayer
  because God can speak to us at different moments
    through persons, events, nature, difficulties,
      even painful situations

God is not limited to our structure and time.
We can help our learners become aware of God's presence
　　by encouraging them to ask:
　　Did I feel especially close to God at any time today?
　　Did I or someone else do something good?
　　When faced with a choice, did I make the right decision?
　　Did I enjoy the beauty of a sunset,
　　　　or a bird, or a tree, and so on?

A Special Place for Prayer

A prayer table in your meeting space is a very easy
　　yet effective way of making prayer
　　　　an integral part of your sessions.
You can arrange it simply: a small table with a candle
　　and a Bible placed on top.
If possible set it in the center of your group's meeting space.
You might have a brief ceremony
　　(a Bible service, for example)
　　　　to "inaugurate" it at the beginning of the year.
Then always share your group prayer gathered around it.
You can arrange the prayer table according to seasons
　　or your prayer theme.
For example, during Advent you can place
　　your Advent wreath on the table.
During Lent you can cover the table with a purple cloth,
　　and place a cross or crucifix on it, or a crown of thorns
　　　　(made by tying a thorny vine in a circlet).
All children, even the young, can help prepare the table.
By involving the children or teens this way,
　　they will feel the table is theirs.
It will truly be a symbol of God's presence,
　　as the ark of the covenant was for the Hebrews.

Other ways to make prayer time more effective
include lighting (use lamps or spotlights instead of
the overhead lights, or use fewer overhead);
music (reflective background music or music for
opening and closing songs);
and prayer mats (carpet remnants, pillows,
pieces of an old blanket, etc.); using incense;
slides or videos appropriate for the season or theme.
Obviously, some of these require more planning and preparation.
If your learners are older children or teens,
you might ask one or two to help you set up.

Our Image of God

Another consideration is involved in the question:
"What is prayer?"
Since prayer is a relationship, our prayer is often shaped
by our image of God, by the way we think of God.
This is true for children as well as adults.
The Hebrew Scriptures reveal God as creator, Lord, leader,
shepherd, tender mother, the holy one,
partner in a covenant, spouse.
Pause for a moment and ask yourself:
"What is my image or concept of God?"
Of course, we know that any image falls short of God's reality.
In fact, our relationship with God is of a very different quality
than any human relationship.
One way of knowing the image of God that most appeals to us
is to ask ourselves:
"When I read the Bible, which are my favorite passages?
What image of God appeals to me?
Which do I turn to most frequently?
What image of God do I, as a catechist,
communicate to my children?"

What image of God do the children or teens you teach
    have of God?
If you teach primary children, you might have them
    draw their own pictures of God, then talk about them.
You could ask them which Bible stories are their favorites and why.
With preteens and teens you could ask what comes to mind
    when they hear or say the word "God."
Encourage them to speak from the heart
    and not worry about a "right" answer.
If they find it difficult to share their thoughts aloud,
    ask them to write down their favorite Scripture passages.
The group could then discuss what images of God
    are found in those passages.
If your learners have negative images of God,
    you'll need to help them address that
    so they will be able to develop
        a loving relationship with God.
Some children may be raised to think of God as a judge,
    the one who rewards and punishes.
We can help these children by speaking of God's love,
    reading Scripture excerpts that speak of God's love for us.
Stress that God loves us no matter what.
    We don't earn God's love; it is freely given.
    We don't have to bargain with God.
Share some of your own experiences.
Another way to help children overcome negative images of God
    is by helping them develop a healthy sense of self-esteem,
        based on their call to an intimate relationship with God.
Our relationship with God is a living, growing one
    that needs to be nurtured and developed.
God reaches out to us first but awaits our response in love.

For Reflection and Discussion

• Prayer is our relationship with God. What does that mean to you? How would you share that experience and understanding with your learners?

• Who are some other persons in the Scriptures whom God called to a special relationship with himself? How might you incorporate their experience of God in a prayer service during your religion session?

• Which are your favorite Scripture passages? What images of God do you find in them? Are there others that appeal to you more?

• How do you image God for your learners?

• What concrete methods can you use to inspire your children or teens to think about and express their idea about prayer? To express their images of God?

Share a Prayer Experience

You can use the following prayer experience
   as a springboard for your own ideas.
Play some soft, reflective background music.
Darken the room to provide the right atmosphere.
Invite the learners to close their eyes
   and breathe slowly and deeply to help them relax.
Use the following or similar words:
Picture yourself in your favorite place,
   a place where you feel happy and safe.
(Pause for a few moments.)
Then picture someone else there with you,
   someone whom you can feel loves you very much.
It's a little hazy, so you can't really see the person's features,
   but you sense that it is God.

As God's image becomes clearer, say in your own words,
   "Here I am, God."
(Invite the children or teens to speak to God
   in silence for a few minutes.
Then read one of the Scripture passages that speaks
   of God's love for us, for example,
   Isaiah 54:5-8, 49:14-16, 43:1-4; Luke 15;
   John 14:18-21, 16:25-28; 1 John 4:7-12.
After the reading allow a few minutes for more silent reflection.)
Now take some time to draw a picture,
   or write a prayer or poem, or write in your journal,
      about what you thought about during this prayer time.
(Give them enough time for this exercise.)
Now let's pray a psalm of thanksgiving together.
(Some examples are psalm 89, 103, or 104.)

CHAPTER TWO

Jesus, Our Model

Jesus is the first and greatest catechist.
So if we want to guide those we teach in developing
   their prayer life, we need to consider his example first of all.
Where and from whom did Jesus himself learn to pray?
One day when I was leafing through the section on prayer
   in the *Catechism of the Catholic Church*,
      this passage drew my attention:
"The Son of God…earns to pray in the words and rhythms
   of the prayer of his people, in the synagogue at Nazareth
      and the Temple of Jerusalem." (#2599)
I have to confess, I hadn't thought much about it before.
   But Jesus was a boy, a teenager, a man of his people,
      religious culture, and time.
What a perfect model he is
   for us as catechists and for our learners.
Sometimes we might think of prayer
   as something detached from our culture and our century.
Instead, these enrich our prayer.
We don't pray as faceless beings but as children of God
   living in an era of great technological advances.

Each of us belongs to a particular family and neighborhood,
   with a personal and family religious history.
We can share that with those we teach.
One Christmas, for example, a catechist brought some special food
   her mother always made at Christmastime.
She and those in her group sang
   one of the family's favorite hymns.

Mary, the Mother of God

"The Son of God…learns to pray from his mother,
   who kept all the great things the Almighty had done
      and treasured them in her heart." (*Catechism*, #2599)
Jesus as a boy and young man needed models of prayer.
Who could be a better teacher than his mother?
While there aren't many words of Mary recorded in the gospel,
   what is recorded shows how much she loved God and others.
When the angel approached her about accepting the role
   as mother of the messiah, she replied,
   "Here I am, the servant of the Lord;
   let it be done to me according to your word." (Lk 1:38)
When Mary was greeted by Elizabeth as "the mother of my Lord,"
   she in turn praised God.
   "My soul glorifies the Lord for he has looked with favor
      on the lowliness of his servant.
   He has brought down the powerful from their thrones,
      and lifted up the lowly.
   He has filled the hungry with good things
      and sent the empty away." (Lk 1:47–48, 52–53)
Ask younger children: who taught you to pray?
   Who taught you your prayers? Which prayers did you learn?
Once a group of sixth graders were studying prayer in the Bible.
They enjoyed drawing parallels between Jesus' prayers
   and Mary's, and talking about the ways they are alike.

For example, as we already saw, when the angel
   brought God's message to Mary, she said,
   "Let it be done to me."
When Jesus was praying in the garden of Gethsemane
   before his passion, he said, "Not as I will but as you want."
One catechist told me that during Holy Week last year,
   the seventh and eighth graders studied a Seder meal.
That was her first experience of the elements
   of that special Jewish family meal.
She marveled at how much our own Sunday liturgy
   resembles the ritual of the Passover celebration,
      which Jesus followed during the Last Supper.
The cups of blessing and the wording of the prayers;
   the sharing of the bread;
   the reading or narration of Scripture:
   Jesus learned all these in the heart of his family.
Jesus' family, his people, and his culture
   all influenced and shaped his prayer.

Jesus and Scripture

Another important part of the culture of Jesus' people
   are the Hebrew Scriptures.
As a boy and young man Jesus would have studied
   the Scriptures and used them in prayer
      at home and in the synagogue.
The Scriptures are an excellent resource
   for teaching children about prayer.
Think of some one-on-one encounters
   between God and individuals
      that we find recorded in the Bible.
In the Hebrew Scriptures we find God calling persons
   to a personal covenant relationship with God.

The response of these individuals—
  whether in word, action, or both—was prayer, an encounter.
The Book of Genesis, for example, narrates the moving story
  of Abraham's faith journey.
  "Now the Lord said to Abram, 'Go from your country
  and your kindred and your father's house
    to the land that I will show you.
  I will make of you a great nation and I will bless you.'
  So Abram went as the Lord had told him." (Gen 12:1–4)
Another example is that of Moses, who first encountered God
  in the burning bush (Ex 3).
  God called to him: "Moses, Moses."
  And Moses said: "Here I am."
He recognized God's presence and responded to God's action
  in his life…sometimes (like most of us) rather imperfectly.
If we look in the gospels we find several instances
  of Jesus' contact with people;
    for example, Jesus' conversation with the Samaritan woman,
      found in chapter four of John's gospel.
Jesus spoke first.
  He drew the woman out and engaged her in dialogue.
This conversation touched the woman so much
    that she left her water jar and ran to tell the townspeople
    about Jesus.
Not only does Scripture offer examples
  of the prayer relationship,
    it contains some of the most profound prayers ever written,
      in particular the psalms in the Old Testament.
The psalms were an important part of the prayer
  of the Jewish people.
Jesus certainly would have known and prayed them daily.
These universal prayers come from the heart and from life,
  yet they transcend human experience.

The psalms speak to almost any situation and need in life.
Psalm 23 ("The Lord is my shepherd") is a favorite, of course.
Other psalms such as 8, 18, 24, and 27 are equally inspired
   and inspiring.
Children generally find it easy to pray with the psalms.
The psalms lend themselves to group, choral,
   or individual prayer; to litany-like prayer;
      and to silent meditation.

In the gospels we find several instances
   of Jesus' knowledge of the Scriptures.
He uses many of the Old Testament images
   for God and his people in the parables he tells:
   for example, the good shepherd caring for his sheep;
   the parable of the owner and his vineyard;
      and the parable of the wedding banquet.
Jesus quotes Scripture in reference to himself:
   "The Spirit of the Lord is upon me,
   because he has anointed me." (Lk 4:18)
With his family, with his people, he would have prayed:
   "Hear, O Israel! The Lord our God, the Lord is one!
   You shall love the Lord your God with all your heart,
   and with all your soul, and with all your strength,
      and with all your mind."
We Christians know this as the first great commandment.
It expresses the core of our relationship with God.

Lectio Divina

One way of using the Scriptures for prayer is called *lectio divina*.
It is basically a way of meditating on Scripture.
We can simplify it for use with those we teach.
The first step is to read a passage from Scripture,
   slowly and reflectively.

Let it speak to you personally.
Then share the words or phrases that strike you the most.
Read the passage again.
If you wish, share any reflections that come to you personally.
Then either offer spontaneous prayers
    based on the Scripture you read,
        or use a prayer formula or intercessory prayer.

Jesus and His Father

Most importantly of all, Jesus' prayer springs
    from a "secret source": his relationship with his Father.
    "Father, I thank you for having heard me.
        I knew that you always hear me." (Jn 11:41–42)
    "I thank you, Father, Lord of heaven and earth,
    because you have hidden these things from the wise
    and the intelligent and have revealed them to infants.
        Yes, Father, for such was your gracious will." (Mt 11:25)
    "Father, the hour has come;… I glorified you on earth
        by finishing the work that you gave me to do." (Jn 17:1, 4)
We can find several of Jesus' own prayers in the gospel
    and use them with our learners.
Sometimes we might use them in litany-like prayers;
    for example, "I thank you, Father, Lord of heaven and earth"
        can be the response.
Older children can write simple mantras based on these prayers.
Mantras are short prayers repeated over and over
    in a reflective way, such as "Jesus, Son of David,
        have mercy on me."
Younger children can be taught to pray these mantras
    when they experience or "feel" God's presence.
Jesus' prayer, as recorded in the gospel, expresses oneness
    with his Father.

The *Catechism* puts it this way: "The whole of Jesus' prayer
is contained in the loving adherence of his human heart
to the mystery of the will of the Father." (#2603)
Isn't this after all the essence of prayer,
of our relationship with God:
loving adherence to the will of the Father?
Jesus prays that he might fulfill that will.
So he is an example for us in this as well.
When he prays, he prays for himself as well as for others.
He prays before the decisive moments of his own mission:
at his baptism; during his forty days of fasting in the desert;
the night before he chose his apostles;
before his transfiguration; at the beginning of his passion.
His prayer is in tune with the Father's heart.
These passages of the gospel are a lesson for us
as well as for those we teach.

Praying for Others

If a young person comes to us outside of our religion session
to talk about a personal problem or concern,
we can pray with them.
We can invite our children to write short prayers
for their own specific needs.
They would be free to share these aloud with the group or not.
A child once wrote: "God, if you hear me, please help.
My parents argue a lot. I think my dad drinks too much.
Help them, God, and help me. I'm not sure what to do."
In the gospel we find that Jesus prays constantly for others:
for his apostles, for those who come to him to be healed,
for the crowds who gather to hear his words,
for his closest friends.
We can use his example to teach our learners to pray for others.

"Jesus took the children in his arms, laid his hands on them,
and blessed them." (Mk 10:16)
Ask younger children to think about how they would feel.
What would they say to Jesus?
Well, Jesus does bless them every day.
"Holy Father, protect them in your name
so that they may be one, as we are one....
Sanctify them in the truth." (Jn 17:11, 17)
Children easily learn to pray for their family and friends.
That's important, especially when situations call for healing,
or in times of special joy.
We can help them broaden their horizons by offering prayers
for persons they may not know,
or persons outside their family circle;
for hungry, homeless children and families;
for victims of a flood, tornado, or earthquake;
for a baby who was just baptized in the parish; and so on.

Lord, Teach Us to Pray

When we learn from Jesus how to pray, we are like the disciples.
They saw Jesus at prayer, and they wanted to learn
to pray as he did.
So they asked him, "Lord, teach us to pray."
And Jesus taught them the Our Father.
In another chapter we will look more closely at this prayer,
which is a catechesis in itself.
Jesus was thus constantly teaching about prayer,
both by word and example.
The parable Jesus told about the persevering woman
and the unjust judge often brings a chuckle.
We can picture the judge muttering, "I'd better give this woman
what she wants before she wears me out!"

Jesus is encouraging us to "wear God out" with our prayers.
When the children I teach complain,
"But I've been praying for so long,"
I tell them about this parable.
Jesus' parables on prayer are simple for children and teens
to act out.
This is an enjoyable way for them to learn and remember
what he taught.
They can also write their own, modern versions,
for example, of the passage from Luke where Jesus speaks
of a friend needing to borrow from another friend
in the middle of the night (Lk 11:5ff).
They usually are eager to act out their parables for their families.
This exercise can help them understand these stories better.
Jesus told another parable about bridesmaids
waiting to celebrate a wedding.
Ten bridesmaids took their lamps
and went to meet the bridegroom.
At midnight there was a shout: "Look!
Here is the bridegroom!
Come out to meet him."
Then all those bridesmaids got up and trimmed their lamps.
While the foolish bridesmaids went to buy oil for their lamps,
the bridegroom came, and those who were ready
went with him into the wedding banquet.
(Adapted from Mt 25:1–12)
We can use this parable also to teach about prayer,
comparing the oil in the lighted lamps to hearts
that have kept close to God through prayer.
Younger children will enjoy acting out the parable
in a simpler version.
We also need to explain to our learners
that Jesus didn't answer people's prayers

because the people were important,
    or had piled up a stockroom of good deeds.
In the gospel he tells us that what he looks for
    is conversion of heart, faith, trust, and watchfulness.
In fact, some of the persons whom Jesus healed
    were looked down on by their "more virtuous" neighbors,
        for example, the lepers, who were outcasts,
        or the Canaanite woman in Matthew's gospel.
Her prayer was simple: "Have mercy on me, Lord, Son of David;
    my daughter is tormented by a demon."
Although the woman was considered an unbeliever,
    Jesus healed her daughter and praised the mother:
        "Woman, great is your faith!" (Mt 15:21–28).
That is real praise, especially coming from Jesus himself.
The words, "Woman of great faith" also make us think of Mary.
On the one hand, she was Jesus' teacher
    and, on the other, his disciple.
We can ask Mary to join her prayer to ours,
    to help us pray with faith and love as she did,
        with loving adherence to the will of the Father.
Older children or teens might do a silent reflection
    or guided meditation on Mary's visit
        to Elizabeth (Lk 1:39–56).
Invite younger children to learn a simple hymn to Mary.
    Or do a very short guided meditation, such as the following.

Do you remember the gospel story about Mary
    going to visit her cousin Elizabeth?
Let's close our eyes and try to picture it.
    Just relax and picture Elizabeth getting ready.
When you know that someone you love is coming to visit you,
    how do you feel?
    Happy and excited? Nervous?

Anxious to have everything right?
Elizabeth probably felt that, but she also felt something more.
She knew Mary was special. Why was Mary special?
   And who is Jesus?
So when Mary arrived, Elizabeth said to her:
   "Blessed are you among women,
   and blessed is the fruit of your womb."
Do these words sound familiar?
   Where have you heard them before?
   (Give the children some clues, if they hesitate.)
That's right, in the Church's prayer the Hail Mary.
Let's say the Hail Mary now and ask Mary to come
   and bring Jesus into our hearts.

For Reflection and Discussion

• Where, how, and from whom did you learn to pray—as a
child, as an adolescent, as an adult?

• List five values you have learned in your family, your neighborhood, your parish, in American culture. In what concrete
ways have these shaped your prayer life? How can you bring
them into your religion sessions?

• How has Jesus figured in your prayer life? Do you consider
him a model of prayer? How and what can you personally
learn from his example?

• Present Jesus to your learners as a model of prayer by using
Jesus' prayers from the gospels. Have the learners write their
own prayers based on Jesus' prayers. Give examples of how
Jesus prayed for others. During your sessions pray for the needs
of others. Be open to talking with your children and teens and
praying with them. Read and discuss some of Jesus' parables
and teachings on prayer. Stress how Jesus listens to our prayers.

Sharing a Prayer Experience

For this prayer experience you may invite the children
   to place on your prayer table something symbolizing
   their relationship with Jesus,
      for example, a lighted candle, incense, a favorite picture.
Suggest that they breathe deeply and let themselves relax
   so they can focus better.
The gospel records many encounters
   between Jesus and individual persons.
Each of them has a unique relationship to him,
   depending on his call to them and their response.
   Some see him as Teacher,
      some as Healer.
   Some see him as the Font of living waters,
      others as their Refuge.
   Some see him as the Light,
      others as the true Friend.
   Still others see him as the Shepherd,
      or as Wisdom.
Tell the participants to pause a moment and ask themselves:
   Which of these images speaks to me at this moment?
   Which can I most relate to?
   (They may have another not mentioned here.)
Think of a gospel passage that exemplifies this relationship.
   For example, for the Font of living water,
      the Samaritan woman at the well speaks with Jesus.
   For Jesus as the Light: Jesus curing the man born blind.
Invite them to picture themselves in the scene with Jesus,
   and to talk to him.
It may be that they just say his name, as Mary Magdalene did
   on Easter morning: "Rabboni: Master."
This is a response of faith.

Conclude with the famous, very personal prayer
   of St. Augustine (*Confessions*, Book X):

Late have I loved you,
O Beauty so ancient and so new,
late have I loved you.
And behold, you were within me
and I was outside, and it was there that I sought you.
You called me, you cried out to me, you shattered my deafness.
You dazzled me, you blinded me,
and you finally healed my blindness.
You breathed upon me your perfume
and I breathed it, and now I gasp for you.
I have tasted you, and now I hunger and thirst for you.
You touched me, and now I yearn for your peace.

CHAPTER THREE

Prayer in the Liturgy

After the ascension of the Lord into heaven,
   the disciples "returned to Jerusalem
      from the mount called Olivet.
   Entering the city they went to the upstairs room
      where they were staying.
   Together they devoted themselves to constant prayer.
   When the day of Pentecost came it found them
      gathered in one place.
   Suddenly from up in the sky came a noise
      like a strong, driving wind which was heard
      all through the house where they were seated.
   Tongues as of fire appeared, which parted
      and came to rest on each of them.
   All were filled with the Holy Spirit."
      (Acts 1:12–14; 2:1–4a)
This same Spirit leads, forms, and inspires the Church
   in her life of prayer in every age.

The Christians in the first community of Jerusalem
    "devoted themselves to the apostles' instruction
    and the communal life, to the breaking of bread
        and the prayers." (Acts 2:42)
These elements characterize the Church's prayer,
    which is, as the *Catechism of the Catholic Church* notes,
    "founded on the apostolic faith, authenticated by charity,
        and nourished in the Eucharist." (#2624)
We will see this very clearly as we look at
    the celebration of the Mass.
The first source of the Church's prayer,
    one we've already discussed,
    is the Word of God, the Scriptures.
What is the first thing we do at Mass, after the Introductory Rites?
Yes, we celebrate the Word of God in the Liturgy of the Word.
Another source of the Church's prayer is found
    in the great liturgical traditions of the Church,
    that is, the history, theology, and development
        of the Church's liturgy.
The formulas of the prayers in the liturgy
    have changed over the years,
    for example, after Vatican II,
        but the forms of prayer remain the same.
The forms are adoration, thanksgiving,
    contrition, and petition.
They lie at the heart of prayer, whether it's in the Bible
    or in the liturgy, or in private, individual prayer.
The *Catechism* words them a bit differently:
    blessing and adoration, petition (includes asking forgiveness),
    intercession, thanksgiving, and praise.
The basics, however, are the same.
There's a rhyme you can use to help your children
    memorize the forms:

In blessing, adoration
Our voices we raise—
Petition, intercession,
Thanksgiving and praise.

We find all these forms expressed in the liturgy,
   particularly in the celebration of the Eucharist.

What Is Blessing?

Blessed are you, Lord of all creation.
Through your goodness we have this bread which we offer you.
Blessed are you, Lord of all creation.
Through your goodness we have this wine which we offer you.
Blessed be God forever!

This blessing expresses the dialogue between God and us
   that is at the heart of prayer.
I bless the Lord, for the Lord has blessed me.
   My blessing is a response to and acceptance of God's gifts.
A child once asked, "How can we bless God?
   I mean, isn't God the one who does the blessing?"
One of the others in the group responded,
   "When I do something for my grandma, she always says,
   'Bless you, dear.' Maybe it's something like that."
In one lesson on prayer, we talked about the different ways
   of blessing someone, and why we say, "Bless the Lord."
The children wanted to write their own blessings,
   and some of them were quite original.
   "Bless you, Lord, for the bees. You're a honey."
   "Bless you, Lord, for pizza."
   "Bless you, Lord, for brother sun and sister moon,
      and the stars and the rain and the wolf and the birds."
Blessings go from us to God
   because blessings come from God to us.

Using our very limited terms we could say
  that our blessings ascend to God.
God's graces and gifts descend to us.
Challenge your learners to find how many times
  the words bless, blessed, or blessing are said
    in the prayers of the Mass.

We Praise and Adore You

Three other forms of prayer rise to God:
  adoration, thanksgiving, and praise.
  "Father, you are holy indeed, and all creation
    gives you praise."
  "Holy, holy, holy, Lord God Almighty."
The Mass, especially the Liturgy of the Eucharist,
  is filled with prayers of adoration,
    thanksgiving, and praise.
They express our belief that God is the one to whom
  we owe everything, including life itself.
In these prayers we adore and praise God for his own sake.
We give God glory, not for what God does,
  but because God is.
Moses asked God, "If the Israelites ask me, 'What is his name?'
  what shall I tell them?"
God said to Moses "I Am Who I Am." (Ex 3:13–14)
In one religion session we had finished a prayer lesson
  on God our Creator.
I asked the children, as part of their prayer, to draw or color
  a picture showing that life comes from God.
At Mass we celebrate the gift of life in many different ways:
  offering the gifts of the earth;
  celebrating the gift of the Spirit;
    remembering the gift of Jesus' life, death, and resurrection.

We want those we teach to always appreciate these gifts.

One catechist asked her eighth grade group how they show
in their lives that they believe God is their Creator.

She said: Ask yourselves, can other people
tell from my actions that I am a believer?

Some of their answers were: I show that I believe in God
by going to church…by other kinds of prayer…
by obeying God's laws…by caring for God's gifts of health
and of the earth…by showing respect for other people…
by helping others.

The children obviously made the connection.

You can ask your learners to write a litany of praise.

Some sample petitions are:

Praise and thanks to you, Lord of sea and sky.

Praise and thanks to you, good Father.

Praise and thanks to you, who made everything.

Praise to you, Jesus our Friend.

Praise to you, Jesus our Savior.

The word "Eucharist" itself means praise and thanksgiving.

The Mass is a living sacrifice of praise, that is,
what we pray, what we celebrate at Mass, are not just words,
are not just a memorial of past events.

The Lord Jesus' offering of himself, and our personal offering
along with his, are what give value to this celebration.

Bless Us, Lord

Two other forms of prayer have to do
with the movement of God's blessing to us.

These are petition and intercession.

When we petition, we pray for the coming of the kingdom.

We pray for all that is necessary to accomplish this,
and for our own needs: for forgiveness, for guidance,
for health, for spiritual growth.

Intercession is a form of petition.
It is prayer for others, as in the General Intercessions
    or Prayer of the Faithful that is part of every liturgy.
Prayers of petition and intercession also form part
    of the Eucharistic Prayer.
        "May we who are fed by his body and blood be filled
        with his Holy Spirit, and become one body in Christ."
We pray for peace in the world.
We ask God to strengthen the faith of the Church,
    its leaders, and all its people.
One way to foster a spirit of prayer for others
    in your children and teens is to use the events of the week
        as a source or springboard for prayer.
Invite your learners to bring in newspaper
    or magazine clippings about persons, events, or situations
        they would like to pray for.
Invite them to place those clippings on your prayer table
    in the middle of your gathering space,
        or make a collage on the bulletin board.

Make the Connection

Children and teens need to see liturgy as related to life,
    not just a "Sunday thing."
You can discuss how it connects to and expresses their daily lives,
    for example, when we offer the bread and wine,
        as well as our monetary offering.
Some catechists have made that connection
    by discussing the different forms of prayer in the Mass.
We can help our children or teens see that we can praise,
    thank, and bless God at any time.
The Mass teaches us how to do this.
    It also shows us how to live in a way that praises God.

At the same time, when we go to Mass,
    we bring all the things that happened during the week
        and offer them to God.
During our religion session, I ask my group to think
    of some of the things they will offer God.
We praise God together for all the good things
    and ask pardon for the times we haven't done God's will.
Studying the symbols and gestures the liturgy uses
    is another means of making the connection:
    the bread and wine, the candles,
        the altar or table of the Lord, the sign of peace,
            kneeling, standing, and so on.
All of these tell us something about what
    we are doing at Mass and how it affects our lives.
Music is a very bonding form of prayer,
    that is, it draws people together and helps form them
        into a community.
This is true for children's music, too.
Silence is another key element in the liturgy,
    in fact, for all prayer experiences.
Reflective silence offers all of us the chance
    to allow God to talk to us,
    to listen to God's voice in the readings,
    in the prayers of the Mass,
    and in the voices and needs of the people around us.
Gestures, symbols, music, silence, and listening—
    we need all of these as elements of our prayers,
    so our prayer will be more alive and fruitful,
    so our prayer experiences with those we teach
        will be more meaningful.
With your learners list some of these elements.
    Then talk about how each one can help us pray better.
The Mass is certainly filled with all these elements.

We've also used several of them in our prayer experiences
in the first two chapters.
(For rituals and prayer services based on the symbols
of the liturgy, refer to *Rites and Rituals* of this series.)
May the liturgy continually nourish, inspire,
and form our prayer life and that of our learners.

For Reflection and Discussion

• What part does the liturgy play in your prayer life? What positive things can you do to help make the liturgy an important part of the prayer life of your children? For example, do you use any of the prayers from the liturgy in your religion lessons, either as models of prayer or as prayer formulas?

• What insights has this chapter offered you with regard to the prayers of the liturgy? Name three concrete ways in which you can apply these insights to your teaching.

• How would you explain the six forms of prayer to your learners in a sentence or two each: blessing, adoration, thanksgiving, praise, petition, intercession?

• How often do you use these in your prayer during your religion sessions: symbols and sacramentals such as candles, pictures, holy water, a crucifix; gestures such as raising hands, bowing, and other prayer postures; silence; listening; rituals; writing or drawing?

Share a Prayer Experience

Our prayer experience will be somewhat different this time.
Invite the children or teens to place on your prayer table
a Bible, a lighted candle, and photos that remind them
of persons and places dear and important to them,

plus magazine and newspaper clippings
of persons and events for whom they feel concern.
Use the following or similar words for the guided meditation.

Play some relaxing music and place yourself
in a comfortable position.
Breathe in and out slowly and feel your body relax.
In silence place yourself in God's presence.
Now, take one of the photos or clippings
and wait in silence for a prayer to come to your heart.
(Pause for some moments of silence, then continue.)
You may express that prayer aloud.
(Encourage them by sharing your own prayer.)
The prayer can be one of praise, thanksgiving, blessing,
petition, or intercession.
Do the same with another photo and/or clipping.
Don't rush your prayers.
Let them spring from the heart.
(Close with any form of prayer you wish,
whether it's spontaneous or a prayer formula
such as the Our Father.)

CHAPTER FOUR

The Lord's Prayer

The Lord's Prayer has been called
    the "compendium of the gospel"
        and "the most perfect of prayers."
One thing that has always struck me is that
    the Our Father is used so often in Christian prayer
        and in so many ways.
The Church's prayer follows a cycle, just as our lives do,
    just as your own prayer probably does.
These rhythms of prayer—daily, weekly, yearly—
    are all marked by the Lord's Prayer.
Our children need to be familiar with them,
    since their prayer life, too, is formed by these rhythms.
You could have the children make a chart of the liturgical year.
Discuss how the Church seasons (Advent, Christmas,
    Lent, Easter, etc.) correspond to the seasons of the year.
Each of the Church seasons is marked by certain prayer themes.

The Liturgy of the Hours

One way of marking the daily rhythms
    is the Liturgy of the Hours.

The Liturgy of the Hours,
    part of the Church's official daily prayer,
        also follows the Church seasons.
The Liturgy has special prayers for different times of the day,
    especially morning and evening.
Plan a prayer service based on the Liturgy of the Hours.
    All the elements should be appropriate
        for the liturgical season you are in.
The structure is
- Invitatory (an opening antiphon such as "Come, let us worship the Lord.")
- Hymn
- Three (or two) antiphons and psalms (the antiphons are like an introduction to the psalms, e.g., the Virgin has given birth to the Savior)
- Reading from Scripture
- Canticle of Mary
- Intercessions
- Our Father
- Closing prayer.

Practice writing a prayer for each season.

On several occasions, I have brought some of the children
    in my religion class to a nearby monastery,
    to share the Liturgy of the Hours with the priests and brothers.
They enjoyed the experience,
    and noticed how every hour closes with the Our Father.
We were talking about the Our Father in one session.
I told the children how the early Christian communities
    prayed the Our Father three times a day,
        in place of the eighteen blessings
            that were part of the Jewish prayer tradition.

Most of the children were very interested,
and some said they wanted to do the same thing.

The "Most Perfect Prayer"

In the daily and Sunday celebration of the Eucharist,
the praying of the Our Father has a key position
after the Consecration and
before receiving Holy Communion.
It is the prayer of the whole Church.
The Our Father sums up all the praise and prayers
that preceded it, and expresses our longing
for the bread of life, the Eucharist.
The Lord's prayer is also an integral part of the other
sacraments of initiation, that is, baptism and confirmation.
The *Catechism of the Catholic Church* says that
"the handing on of the Lord's Prayer signifies new birth
into the divine life." (#2769)
The Our Father is one of the "gifts" catechumens receive
during Lent, before they are baptized.
If the Church gives such a prominent position
to the Our Father, teaching it to our learners should be
an essential part of their formation in prayer.
The Our Father teaches us and our children priorities
in our prayer, in our relationship with God,
and in our daily choices.
St. Thomas Aquinas wrote that
"the Lord's Prayer is the most perfect of prayers.
In it we ask, not only for all the things we can rightly desire,
but also in the sequence that they should be desired."
An activity you can do with any age group
is to look at the Our Father and ask:
What do we ask for first? second? third? (and so on).

Another compelling reason, of course,
    for giving importance to the Our Father in our catechesis
    is that it comes to us from Jesus himself,
    the first and greatest Catechist
        and the model of our prayer.
In the Our Father Jesus gives us the words
    the Father gave him.
Because he knows the needs of his brothers and sisters,
    he reveals them to us in this prayer.
While the Our Father is a vocal prayer, it also lends itself easily
    to meditation and even to contemplative prayer.
For example each year, for a series of eight weeks,
    our religion group used the Our Father as the focal point
        and springboard of our prayer.

Calling God by Name

In the first three petitions we do not even mention ourselves.
We focus on the God we love, and we pray for God's glory.
We can become so used to the words
    "Our Father who art in heaven," that we take them for granted.
    But when we stop to think about it, it's astounding.
Jesus taught us to call God "Father," actually "Abba,"
    which means "Daddy."
    So we share in some way in Jesus' relationship with his Father.
The Holy Spirit enables us to pray this way.
Teach your children or teens to frequently find a quiet place
    and say, over and over,
        "Our Father who art in heaven."
    This practice helps us remember who we are
    and where we came from,
        from whom we came, and how much God cares for us.
The reasons for our stress or anxiety become less important
    and are put into perspective.

We can also pray this phrase with our learners as a group.
Jesus himself revealed the Father's name to us.
The name Father transcends any paternal or maternal images,
    any names we may come up with in human terms.
We need to explain to our learners—
    perhaps even to ourselves—that words we use for God
        are only our inadequate way of naming the mystery of God.
I once asked the children in my group what they thought of
    when they prayed the words "Our Father,"
        how they felt about using them.
Their answers varied: "I feel secure."
    "I think of someone who looks out for me."
    "I want to know more about God."
We talked about how they relate to their families as children.
We agreed that when we love someone very much,
    we try to be like them, act, talk, even dress like them.
We trust them and trust that they will act for our good.
    Then we applied this to our relationship with God.

Another catechist said that when he talks about prayer
    and trust in God with his learners,
        he likes to illustrate two extremes with stories.
One extreme of prayer and trust is to leave everything to God
    without making any effort ourselves.
He tells this story about a man sitting on top
    of his house in a flood.
    Some friends came along and asked him to come
    to safety with them, but he answered,
    "No, God will save me from the flood."
    The same thing happened when a boat,
        then a helicopter came.
    When the waters rose and the man drowned,
        he found himself at the gates of heaven.

He saw the Lord and said, "I trusted you would save me
from the flood, but here I am."
The Lord replied, "I sent your friends, a boat,
and a helicopter. What more did you want?"

With the words "Our Father," we call on God;
we place ourselves in God's presence.
This is something we do—or should do—
every time we pray.
But we know that prayer is not a panacea,
an automatic "fix-it."
Prayer is really a relationship, a dialogue,
not just a recitation of words.
We need to live what we pray.
We don't try to analyze our words when we pray,
any more than a couple tries to analyze
their expressions of love for each other.

Honor God's Name in Our Lives

When I was young, the phrase "Hallowed be thy name"
made me think of Halloween.
I wondered what it meant and what the connection was.
Then I learned that "Halloween" comes from
"All Hallows Eve," that is, the eve of All Saints Day.
"Hallowed," therefore, must have something to do
with being called holy, with being treated as holy.
If you have older children, ask them to find
passages in the Bible that speak of or refer to God's holiness.
Some of the most common ones are:
Moses and the burning bush:
"Remove the sandals from your feet for the place
where you stand is holy ground." (Ex 3:5)

The call of Isaiah: "Holy, holy, holy
    is the Lord of hosts!" (Is 6:3)
Mary's canticle: "God who is mighty has done great things
    for me; holy is his name." (Lk 1:49)
When we pray, "Hallowed be thy name,"
    we are praying that God and God's name
        be respected and treated as holy.
We need to teach our learners that this depends
    on our lives and our prayer.
A holy teacher of the Church, St. Peter Chrysologus said,
    "We ask God to hallow his name, which by its own holiness
        saves and makes holy all creation….
    The name of God should be hallowed in all our actions."
Talk about this with your children or teens.
How can we hallow God's name in our actions?
One of the most powerful proofs of God's presence and holiness
    is found in the lives of God's holy people,
        both past and present.
My children love to learn about the saints
    and contemporary Christian witnesses like
        Mother Teresa of Calcutta and Archbishop Oscar Romero.

What Would Jesus Do?

The lives of these holy people also exemplify the fulfillment
    of the next two petitions:
    "Thy kingdom come, thy will be done
        on earth as it is in heaven."
"Thy kingdom come" refers first of all
    to Christ's second coming, which will bring
        the fulfillment of God's reign.
It also refers to the daily coming of Christ
    into the lives and hearts of men and women,
        and through them into the world.

The Holy Spirit forms each person in the image of Christ.
When the children in my religion class asked me
    where God's kingdom is,
        I explained it is not a place but a way of living.
We prayed together to let God have first place in our lives.
Then we prayed that God would be first in our families,
    our neighborhood, our country, and our world.
All this comes about through the action of the Holy Spirit.
Sometimes we think becoming holy depends on our efforts.
However, it is God who acts in us and gives us the gifts
    to grow in God's life, to become better disciples of Jesus.
God's kingdom and will are a mystery we certainly can't fathom.
    But we believe that Jesus gave himself up
    and fulfilled the will of his Father in himself.
He is our example in this as well.
How can we communicate the idea of "God's kingdom"
    and the will of God to our learners?
One way is to pose age-appropriate situations to them,
    situations that require them to make choices.
Challenge them to ask themselves: "What would Jesus do?"
    That question usually brings a variety of responses.
Try to make each of these exercises a prayerful experience,
    not just an intellectual exercise.
For example, if you're discussing a conflict between loyalty
    and honesty, you might ask,
        "If Jesus had a friend who had stolen something
        and another person was being blamed, what would Jesus do?"
Some of the children might say he would talk to his friend
    and convince him either to return what he took
        or to admit his guilt.
A few might say Jesus would stick by his friend no matter what.
Others might say Jesus would go to someone in authority,
    such as a parent or teacher.

Ask each of your learners to search his or her heart
  for a good solution.

Pray for Our Daily Bread

"Give us this day our daily bread."
When we pray these words, we are trusting God
  to show us solutions to personal, local,
  and world problems and sins:
  physical and spiritual hunger, injustice,
  unemployment, poverty, homelessness, disease,
    and, worst of all, despair.
One youth ministry group prepared a collage on the theme:
  Give Us This Day Our Daily Bread.
They showed all kinds of needs and hungers
  and what people were doing about them.
Each week they identified one need that they saw
  in themselves, in their families,
  in the country, and in the world.
They prayed together to ask what realistically they could do
  to alleviate that need.
Sometimes they decided on a group project,
  such as helping serve a meal in a soup kitchen.
Other times they decided to address personal needs
  through sacrifice or a change of attitude.
Praying for our daily bread is important.
We are all bombarded with messages of every kind, every day.
Some of these messages can confuse our sense
  of values and priorities.
They can cloud our consciences,
  so we need God's word, God's life, the Eucharist.
Pray for the spiritual needs of everyone,
  especially for those who don't know they have needs.

Ask for Forgiveness

One spiritual need we all have is for
> forgiveness and reconciliation.

In the next petition of the Our Father we pray for that gift.
> But Jesus added a kind of conditional clause: as we forgive.

One of the most perfect and beautiful pictures of forgiveness
> is the parable of the prodigal son—
> not because the son asks for forgiveness,
> but because his father has already forgiven him
>> without being asked.

Some learners—as well as adults—
> have a difficult time
> believing in this unconditional forgiveness of God.

They have often been taught—
> consciously or unconsciously—
> to see God as judge, the authoritarian teacher,
>> someone who wants an eye for an eye, a favor for a favor.

We think of God in terms of human relationships,
> human justice, and human ways of acting.

This petition raises one of the most problematic issues
> we face in daily life: it's hard to forgive others,
>> even harder to forgive ourselves.

Most of all to accept forgiveness, especially from God,
> challenges our pride.

We need to remind our learners that we ask to be forgiven
> as we forgive others.

We only need to look at Jesus' example.

The gospels describe so many of his acts of forgiveness:
> the Samaritan woman at the well;
>> the woman caught in adultery; the man crippled from birth;
>>> above all, his forgiveness of those who crucified him.

You might choose to share guided meditation with your learners
> on one of these passages.

Depend on God

In the final two petitions, we ask God to keep us
   from all evil and wrongdoing.
A pure, prayerful heart and openness to God's love
   will enable us to distinguish between what is really good
      and what appears to be good.
Of course, we can't trust in our own strength and wisdom.
This is the intention of the final petitions.
Communicating a sense of complete dependence on God—
   especially in our country, with its ideals and heritage
   of freedom, self-reliance, and hard work—
      can be a challenge.
This dependence means that we can't accomplish anything
   on our own, that all we have and are comes from God,
      including the avoidance of evil and the desire to do good.
Perhaps the best way of teaching this
   is through our example,
      through the prayer experiences we have in our sessions,
      especially reflecting on the gospel passages that speak of trust.
Our sense of dependency on God is nourished by
   and inspires our prayer life.
The closer we grow to God, the more we realize
   how dependent we are.
This spirit permeates the Lord's Prayer.

For Reflection and Discussion

   • What place does the Our Father have in your personal prayer?
   Where and when does the Church use the Our Father in liturgical prayer? What does this tell us about its importance?
   • How often do you use the Our Father—in whole or in part—
   in your religion sessions? Have you talked about the meaning
   of the petitions?

- Do you feel comfortable praying to God as "Our Father"? How can you help yourself and your learners understand and appreciate this name of God that Jesus revealed to us?
- What is your understanding of the words, "Give us this day our daily bread"? How can you and your children or teens apply them concretely in your local situation?
- Do you find it difficult to accept God's unconditional forgiveness? To offer that kind of forgiveness to others? How can you help yourself and your learners grow in acceptance and the spirit of reconciliation?
- If you have older children or teens, invite them to prepare a brief prayer service that centers on the Our Father. Have them think about the following: What will your focus be? What elements—gestures, symbols, silence, music, and so on—will you use? Will you use the guided meditation format, or spontaneous prayer, or silent reflection, or a combination of these and other types of prayers?

Share a Prayer Experience

For this prayer experience invite the children or teens
to place some symbols of the Our Father on the prayer table,
such as a candle, incense, a Bible, a nature scene,
a loaf of bread, a picture of needy children, and so on.
You might play reflective music.
After you have all placed yourself in God's presence,
slowly pray the Our Father, pausing in between the petitions.
Tell the learners not to make this an exercise of their minds.
They should just let images, feelings, and thoughts come,
and remain open to them.
After some moments of reflective silence, invite the children
or teens to share their reflections.

Close with a prayer of intercession, such as the following:

Leader	We pray for the Church, her leaders, and all her members, that they may grow in love for the head of the Church, Jesus Christ.
Response	Lord, hear our prayer.
Leader	We pray for the needy of the world, especially families and children, that they may receive what they require to care for their bodies and spirits.
Response	Lord, hear our prayer.
Leader	We pray for ourselves that we may be reconciled with God and one another, and grow in holiness.
Response	Lord, hear our prayer.
Leader	May God the Father bless us through the action of the Spirit. We ask this through Jesus his Son.
All	Amen.

CHAPTER FIVE

Prayer Treasury

A book on prayer or about guiding others in prayer would be
    incomplete without some prayer formulas.
You can use these with your learners as they are,
    as part of a prayer service, or as mantras.
The prayers of the saints are a fine way
    to introduce your learners to these Christian witnesses.

The Lord's Prayer

Our Father, who art in heaven,
hallowed be thy name.
Thy kingdom come, thy will be done
on earth as it is in heaven.
Give us this day our daily bread
and forgive us our trespasses
as we forgive those who trespass against us.
And lead us not into temptation
but deliver us from evil. Amen.

The Hail Mary

Hail Mary, full of grace, the Lord is with thee.
Blessed art thou among women
and blessed is the fruit of thy womb, Jesus.
Holy Mary, Mother of God, pray for us sinners
now and at the hour of our death. Amen.

Glory Be

Glory to the Father, and to the Son, and to the Holy Spirit,
as it was in the beginning, is now, and will be forever. Amen.

The Apostles Creed

I believe in God, the Father Almighty,
creator of heaven and earth.
I believe in Jesus Christ his only Son our Lord.
He was conceived by the Holy Spirit
and born of the Virgin Mary.
He suffered under Pontius Pilate,
was crucified, died, and was buried.
On the third day he rose again.
He ascended into heaven
and is seated at the right hand of the Father.
He will come again to judge the living and the dead.
I believe in the Holy Spirit, the holy Catholic Church,
the communion of saints, the forgiveness of sins,
the resurrection of the body, and life everlasting. Amen.

Prayer of St. Thérèse of Lisieux

Love is what I ask for.
I know only one thing, to love you, Jesus.

Prayer of St. Francis of Assisi

I beg you, Lord, that the strength of your love,
  burning and sweet, may absorb my soul.

Prayer of St. Elizabeth Ann Seton

Jesus, be my Way, Truth, and Life.
Sustain me, Bread of heaven, through the desert of this world,
  until I see you unveiled in glory.

Prayer of St. Patrick

May Christ be with me and Christ be before me.
May Christ be behind me and Christ be within me.
May Christ be below me and Christ be above me.
May Christ be on my right side and Christ on my left.

Prayer of St. Catherine of Siena

O tender Father, you have given me much more
  than I ever thought to ask for.
Our human desires cannot ever equal all
  that you long to give us.

Prayer of St. Maximilian Kolbe

O eternal God, you have loved me before the centuries began.
You have always loved me and you shall always love me!

Prayer of St. Edith Stein

Bless the hearts of all, O Lord,
  especially those who are confused and troubled.
Heal those who are ill, and give peace to tortured souls.

Prayer of St. Bernadette

O Jesus, I no longer feel my cross when I think of yours.